MORMONISM

by
WALTER MARTIN, Ph.D.

Director, Christian Research Institute
Visiting Professor of Comparative
Religions and Apologetics
Melodyland School of Theology
Anaheim, California

D0875007

BETHANY HOUSE PUBLISHERS
Minneapolis, Minnesota 55438
A Division of Bethany Fellowship, Inc.

Revised cover, 1984

Mormonism
Walter Martin

ISBN 0-87123-367-3

Published by Bethany House Publishers
A Division of Bethany Fellowship, Inc.
6820 Auto Club Road, Minneapolis, Minnesota 55438

Printed in the United States of America

Preface

The Church of Jesus Christ of Latter Day Saints, with headquarters in Salt Lake City, Utah, is the official name of the sect known as Mormonism, one of the most original of all American religious movements and one of the most rapidly multiplying of all *non-Christian* cults.

As is the case with most cults, Mormonism claims its special revelations from God, sacred oracles in the form of three volumes (*Book of Mormon, Pearl of Great Price, Doctrine and Covenants*), and a line of "genuine" prophets descended from Joseph Smith and Brigham Young, the first princes, so to speak, of the Mormon hierarchal system.

This booklet is designed chiefly as an introductory survey of the Mormon religion, showing its origin and development, some of its doctrines and its activities, and includes a refutation of certain phases of the system based upon historic biblical theology as directly compared with primary quotations from recognized Mormon authorities.

It is the desire of the author to arouse the Christian Church to the tremendous gains being made today by the numerous *non-Christian* sects in the United States and on every foreign mission field of the world. That there might be a genuine rededication then to the task of Christian apologetics and cult evangelism in this needy field in the defense of Jesus Christ's Gospel is my earnest prayer. With this thought paramount in mind we release this booklet, ever mindful of the responsibility of those who name the name of Christ to not only preach His Gospel but to "reprove, rebuke, exhort with all long-suffering and doctrine" those who after the working of Satan "wrest the scriptures to their own destruction."

Walter Martin

Contents

Chapter One

    The Checkered History of Mormonism 5

Chapter Two

    Examining the Mormon Gospel 14

Chapter Three

    The Mormon Masquerade 20

    Conclusion 30

    Bibliography 31

The Checkered History of Mormonism

In the first chapter of his epistle to the Galatians the Apostle Paul made the following statement:

> I marvel that ye are so soon removed from him that called you into the grace of Christ unto another gospel: Which is not another; but there be some that trouble you, and would pervert the gospel of Christ. But though we, or an angel from heaven, preach any *other gospel* unto you than that which we have preached unto you, let him be *accursed.* As we said before, so say I now *again,* If any man preach any *other gospel* unto you than that ye have received, let him be accursed (Gal. 1:6-9).

This unusual statement by the inspired apostle becomes even more amazing when one stops to realize that the sect today known as Mormonism is apparently a direct fulfillment of the Pauline warning voiced in the first chapter of Galatians. On the night of September 21, 1823, one Joseph Smith, Jr., a resident of New York, allegedly received a visit from an angelic personage, named Moroni, who pronounced himself "a messenger sent from the presence of God," and further that the god whom he represented had work for Joseph Smith to do. [1] Basing his claim to divine inspiration as a prophet of God upon this experience and other experiences he allegedly had with the members of the Trinity, Joseph Smith, Jr., treasure hunter, "peep stone" gazer, and "seer," set out to pen a new revelation now known as *The Book of Mormon,* which is indeed "another gospel" purported by Smith's followers of today (Mormons) to be the "restoration" of the true Gospel of Christ which they contend has for

---

[1] *Pearl of Great Price*, J. S. 2:29-33.

centuries been suppressed by the clergy of all religions in Christendom, a fact which necessitated divine intervention and the anointing of "Prophet" Smith.

Born on the 23rd day of December, 1805, in the little town of Sharon, [2] Vermont, Joseph Smith, Jr., the third son of a family of nine children, had at an early age gained a reputation something less than enviable, to say the least, and he is best understood in the light of the statement made by those who knew him best, his neighbors.

> At this period in the life and career of Joseph Smith, or "Joe Smith," as he was universally named .... he is distinctly remembered as a dull-eyed, flaxen-haired, prevaricating boy, ... by reason of the extravagancies of his statement, his word was received with the least confidence by those who knew him best. He could utter the most palpable exaggeration or marvelous absurdity with the utmost apparent gravity (Pomeroy Tucker, *Origin, Rise and Progress of Mormonism,* p. 16, 1867, New York). [3]

In addition to this statement by Mr. Tucker, the following statement was signed by some sixty-two residents of Palmyra, New York, where the Smiths lived for some time. It cannot be impeached by any honest historian— and it certainly has never been disproved by any Mormons as attested by history:

> We, the undersigned, have been acquainted with the Smith family for a number of years, while they resided near this place. We have no hesitation in saying that we consider them destitute of that moral character which ought to entitle them to the confidence of any community. They were particularly famous for visionary projects; spent much of their time in digging for money which they pretended was hid in the earth, and a large excavation may be seen in the earth not far from their residence where they used to spend their time in digging for hidden treasures. Joseph Smith, Sr., and his son, Joseph, were in particular considered entirely destitute

---

[2] Or Royalton, Vt.

[3] Tucker is vilified by Mormon writers but his facts have never been refuted by non-Mormon contemporaries.

of moral character and addicted to vicious habits (E. D. Howe, *Mormonism Unveiled,* Zanesville, Ohio, 1834, p. 261). [4]

Much more could be said, all of it drawn from primary sources concerning the character and early life of Joseph Smith, up to and including the time when he supposedly was commissioned by the Lord to "restore" the true Gospel of Christ to Christendom. However, I have covered this aspect of the subject thoroughly in my book *The Maze of Mormonism,* [5] where supplementary material carefully documented is available if the interested reader wishes to pursue the subject further.

Returning to the Mormons and their history, some interesting facts should be noted concerning their development.

After his reception of the angel Moroni's threefold visit, Prophet Smith, by angelic authority, approximately three years after the event previously mentioned occurred, supposedly unearthed what he claimed were "golden plates" on which was inscribed in "Reformed Egyptian Hieroglyphics" what has become *The Book of Mormon.*

In addition to this marvelous discovery the considerate angel also directed the prophet to a mysterious pair of "spectacles" entitled Urim and Thummim, respectively, which when the prophet gazed through them, translated the "Reformed Egyptian Hieroglyphics" into English so that Smith was able to transcribe them through his loyal secretaries, Martin Harris and Oliver Cowdery, both of whom in company with one David Witmer swore to the authenticity of Smith's revelation and the existence of the golden plates.

Attention should be called at this point to the fact that both David Witmer and Oliver Cowdery were excommunicated from the Mormon faith as was Martin Harris, and these supposedly unimpeachable witnesses to

---

[4] Howe was a contemporary of Smith and did the most thorough job of research on the Mormon prophet and his religion; his work is today considered *prima facie* evidence of the highest veracity.

[5] Vision House Publishers, Revised and Enlarged, 1976.

the veracity of Smith's revelation were described by their former brethren as "thieves," "liars" and "counterfeiters." [6] This is hardly a staunch recommendation for the veracity of their testimony where *The Book of Mormom* is concerned.

Incidentally, Martin Harris, a prosperous farmer, who befriended Smith and invested money in his schemes, later changed his testimony relative to having viewed the miraculous "golden plates." Said Harris, "Well, I did not see them just as I see the penholder, but I saw them with the eye of faith. I saw them as plainly as I see anything whatever about me, although at the time they were covered over with a cloth" (*Gleanings By the Way,* 1842, Philadelphia, Rev. J. A. Clark). [7]

Today anyone interested in the carefully erected myth concerning the "golden plates" can visit Palmyra, New York, and see the hill Cumorah, where a solitary shaft of granite commemorates the "fact" that it was here that Joseph Smith, the Mormon prophet, discovered the "golden plates" which formed the basis for *The Book of Mormon,* a unique volume which we shall take up a little farther on in this booklet.

On April 6, 1830, at Fayette, New York, the Church of Jesus Christ of Latter Day Saints was officially founded with a membership of thirty souls. As the year 1831 drew to a close, the new church numbered several hundred members, and shortly thereafter relocated in Kirtland, Ohio, sending missionaries soon to Jackson County, Missouri, the supposed location of the marvelous city of Zion to be built in the future according to Mormon interpretations of prophecy obtaining at that time. All did not go well with the saints, however, in Missouri, and in 1833 the Mormons were routed from Jackson County, having stirred up the populace against them "partly on account

---

[6] *The Story of the Mormons* (W. A. Linn, N.Y., 1901, p. 81).

[7] Rev. Clark knew Joseph Smith and his family well, a fact which compelled him to speak out against the Mormon "gospel" and its alleged "prophet."

of their religion and partly because they were abolitionists from the North.''

For a short period of time Mormon refugees sustained themselves in Clay County, Missouri, but increasing opposition to their presence resulted in their expulsion in 1839.

Returning to Illinois in 1839, the Mormons built the city of Nauvoo in Hancock County, and with the help of a charter granted to them by the State Legislature they erected well over 2,000 homes, a temple and many other edifices.

During this period of Mormon history things generally seemed to go well for the "saints" until 1844 when a number of apostate Mormons founded a newspaper called "The Nauvoo Expositor" in which they vigorously attacked the "Prophet" or "General" Smith, as he was fond of being called during this period. This incident incited an uprising which resulted in the destruction of the newspaper and brought about Smith's subsequent imprisonment in June of 1844, at Carthage, Illinois. On June 27, 1844, a vile deed was perpetrated in Carthage upon the person of Joseph Smith and his brother, Hyrum, who while allegedly under the protection of the Governor of the State, were brutally shot to death by an irate mob who stormed the jail and martyred the Mormon prophet and his brother.

As can well be imagined tremendous friction was generated between the Mormons at Nauvoo and the general populace of Illinois; so much so that in 1846 the Mormons abandoned Nauvoo and pushed on to Iowa under the leadership of Brigham Young, Smith's successor, and at length arrived on July 24, 1847, in what has come to be known as the Valley of the Great Salt Lake, in Utah. [8]

Under the iron leadership and creative energy of Brig-

---

[8] A dissident group called the Reorganized Church of Jesus Christ LDS which now allegedly numbers approximately 1,000,000 members, split with Young and went to Independence, Mo., where they still maintain their headquarters.

ham Young, the Mormons eked out of the desert a fruit-
ful existence, and as the years passed Mormonism flour-
ished in the Salt Lake Valley, as did polygamy which
was instituted by Smith in Nauvoo and practiced by the
hierarchy of the Mormon Church, which gradually passed
it down through the ranks, so to speak, until it became
a common practice. [9]

In 1877 Brigham Young yielded to the icy hand of death
and the mantle of Mormon leadership, the presidency
of the church, was assumed by John Taylor, a close as-
sociate of Joseph Smith who himself had been wounded
during the Carthage, Illinois, assassination of the prophet.
President Taylor himself died in 1887 and Wilford Woodruff succeeded to the presidency. It was under the leadership of Woodruff in 1890 that the famous "manifesto"
against the practice of polygamy was issued, a manifesto
which was energized chiefly by the fact that Utah was
forbidden entrance into the Union unless said immoral
practice was abolished. Upon the death of Woodruff, Lor-
enzo Snow became president, and the line of succeeding
presidents continues to this day, the present president
being Kimball.

Regarding the practice of polygamy, it was openly
practiced as early as 1852 and despite the enactment of
a law by Congress in 1862 against the practice little was
done about it until 1890. In 1884 the Supreme Court of
the United States upheld the law against plural marriage,
a decision which brought about the imprisonment of over
a thousand Mormons and the disincorporation of the
Church of Jesus Christ of Latter Day Saints, a confisca-
tion of its property and other penalties imposed by the
Federal Government. It was in the light of this drastic
occurrence that President Woodruff in 1890 issued his
famous manifesto, a manifesto directly contradictory to
the express words of Prophet Smith (*Doctrine and Covenants*, 132:4 and 52) previously held to be infallible ut-
terances from the throne room of God. This inconsistency

---

[9] See Linn, previously cited, pp. 272-281.

has never been successfully explained by the Mormon Church and there can be little doubt that they will continue to maintain such a hesitancy in the light of all of the facts.

To dismiss any doubt as to the veracity of this statement the reader is referred to the book, *Doctrine and Covenants*, section 132, verses 3, 4, 6, 28, 61, 62, an official revelation by Joseph Smith, wherein the prophet states, "Behold I reveal unto you a new and everlasting covenant and if ye abide not in that covenant then are ye damned, for no one can reject this covenant and be permitted to enter into my glory."

Smith goes on in this particular section to state that this new covenant is polygamy, a practice he both originated and openly enjoyed for some time prior to his assassination. *

In direct contradiction to this statement in *Doctrine and Covenants,* the Book of Mormon speaks out most pointedly *against* polygamy (see Jacob, chapter 2, verses 23 and 24) and states that polygamy in the sight of the Lord "was abominable." It therefore appears that *The Book of Mormon* and *Doctrine and Covenants* are a bit at odds with each other despite the fact that both are supposed to be equal parts of the "everlasting gospel," or so Smith states (*History of the Church,* Vol. I, p. 12 compare with *Doctrine and Covenants,* Sec. 20, vv. 8, 9). The problem then is, which revelation should be believed? And to complicate matters even further, in the 1835 edition of *Doctrine and Covenants* an inspired message stated: "Insomuch as this church of Christ has been reproached with the crime of fornication, and polygamy: we declare that we believe, that one man should have one wife; and one woman but one husband, except in case of death, when either is at liberty to marry again

---

* Woodruff, in his letter to the U.S. Government, admitted that polygamy *was* celestial marriage and abolished the practice despite the divine edict of Joseph Smith. He himself and other early Mormons, however, secretly practiced it and he was convicted and fined by the government a few years later for violating his own manifesto.

. . . " (*Doctrine and Covenants,* Sec. 101).

To sum up our comments on this subject we quote from the informative, documented tract "Mormonism, Can It Stand Investigation?" [10] "Although the revelation was recorded by the Church on July 12, 1843, publication of the revelation was not made until August 29, 1852, at a church conference by Orson Pratt" (*Journal of Discourses* 1:53ff.).

However, twenty-three years *after* the "revelation" and *fourteen* after the publication of the "revelation," during which time polygamy was practiced, the 1866 edition of *Doctrine and Covenants* stated that "polygamy was a crime" (*Doctrine and Covenants*, Sec. 109).

The reader is urged to pursue this subject further by obtaining the excellent material offered by the Utah Christian Mission where primary source material is obtainable on Mormonism, in simple, concise and thoroughly documented form.

Throughout the history of Mormonism, then, violence has played a great part. At one time or another the Mormons were "in rebellion against the United States of America," "guilty of the practice of polygamy," "driven from state to state like hunted criminals," and finally "deprived of all their earthly possessions" by a sovereign act of the United States Government, an act which was only revoked after Mormon polygamy was abolished by the aforementioned Woodruff decree in 1890.

One other controversy which plagued the Mormons occurred in 1857 when "the most frightful act of violence in the history of the Mormons—the massacre of 150 non-Mormon immigrants at Mountain Meadows by a band of Mormons and Indians under the lead of Bishop John D. Lee"(Schaff-Herzog, *Encyclopedia of Religious Knowledge,* Vol. VIII, p. 17).

Twenty years after the commitment of this heinous crime John D. Lee was imprisoned, tried, convicted and eventually executed by the Government of the United States for his part in the terrible proceedings of 1857.

---

[10] Utah Christian Mission, Box 1743, Phoenix, Arizona.

Brigham Young himself could claim no clean slate in the matter of the Mountain Meadows massacre, for in his irrefutable book, *The Confessions of John D. Lee,* the former Mormon Bishop (who, it is reputed, later found the Lord Jesus Christ as his Saviour) laid the crime on Brigham Young's doorstep, all violent Mormon denials to the contrary notwithstanding. This testimony is *prima-facie* evidence and cannot be fairly impugned. He had, in his own words, "resigned" himself to what was a just reward for a terrible crime, and only wanted the record set straight. According to Lee, then, Brigham Young authorized the Mountain Meadows massacre and did not lift one finger to prevent it, a crime for which he has long since answered before the judgment bar of the one just Judge.

Concluding this brief survey of Mormon history it is wise to bear in mind that the Mormon cult of today is a far cry from its early progenitors. Mormonism in our age is a well-organized, smoothly run, religio-economic enterprise, and the Mormons besides internally controlling the sugar beet industry of the United States own vast areas in the State of Utah, and for that matter shares in the agricultural and industrial empires of American business. Numbering over 3,500,000,[11] the Utah church continues to grow at a phenomenal rate and boasts such political and economic luminaries as Ezra Taft Benson, Marriot (of the Marriot motor lodges) and George Romney, as well as Ivy Baker Priest. Benson was Secretary of Agriculture, George Romney was President of American Motors and Mrs. Priest was Secretary of the Treasury. The Church of Jesus Christ of Latter Day Saints requires of its young members, that each young member support himself during a two-year missionary tour of duty, and today on most foreign mission fields throughout the world Mormons can be found propagating that "other gospel" of which the Apostle Paul spoke, the gospel of Joseph Smith and Brigham Young.

---

[11] According to *Ensign* magazine, May, 1976.

CHAPTER TWO

Examining the Mormon Gospel

In this chapter, by necessity, we shall confine ourselves to a discussion of *The Book of Mormon* and the Mormon doctrines of the (1) atonement and (2) salvation. In chapter 3 we shall comment upon the historic Mormon doctrines of the trinity, the virgin birth of Christ and the inspiration and authority of the Bible.

THE BOOK OF MORMON

As has been observed in chapter 1, the Mormon "Bible," *The Book of Mormon,* is placed by the Mormons on a parity with the Scriptures of the Old and New Testaments. In the light of this claim we shall now examine some of the internal evidence from the book itself to see if the Mormon position can stand the test of criticism.

According to Mormon teaching, *The Book of Mormon* is an historical outline of the activities of a race of people called the Jaradites, allegedly one of the races who were scattered by the avenging hand of God in the wake of the great confusion of tongues which took place at the tower of Babel (Gen. 11).

The Jaradites allegedly set foot in this hemisphere more than 2,200 years before Christ. A later expedition arrived about 600 B.C. under the Jewish leader Lehi and later divided into two tribes, the Nephites and Lamanites, who promptly went to war with each other and kept up a sort of running battle until the year A.D. 385, when according to *The Book of Mormon,* somewhere in the vicinity of the hill Cumorah in Palmyra, New York, the Lamanites almost completely destroyed the Nephites. Only two dozen souls survived the holocaust. The Lamanites, it should be noted, were cursed by God for their apostasy from the true religion, that is, their skin became dark—at least such is the claim advanced by *The Book of Mormon.*[1] The Book of Moses, contained in the Pearl of Great Price also claims that Cain's curse for the murder of his brother Abel was the mark of the black skin and was perpetuated through his descendants. The Book of Abraham[2] defines these people as "all the Egyptians" (Ab. 1:20-27).

Of the twenty-four persons who survived the miniature Armageddon at Cumorah was Mormon, a direct descendant of Lehi, the founder of the Nephites, and Mormon's son, Moroni. *The Book of Mormon* goes on in great detail to point out how Mormon recorded on plates of gold the previously recounted "historical" events, and states that these plates were entombed in the neighborhood of Palmyra, N.Y., about 420 A.D. in the very hill Cumorah where Joseph Smith, Jr., almost 1400 years later unearthed them through the miraculous intercession of Mormon's long-dead son, Moroni, the informative angel of Smith's midnight visitation. It appears that Moroni had managed somehow to progress from a man to the rank of an angel over a period of fourteen centuries, an unbiblical view, to say the least, and another problem Mormon theologians have never fully answered.

The interesting thing about this amazing record contained in *The Book of Mormon* is the fact that within the very pages of this same volume are numerous direct *plagiarisms* from the Authorized Version of the Bible, which did not come into existence as a translation from the Greek until over 1,000 years later than the claimed date of *The Book of Mormon.*

One of these plagiarisms, which is most embarrassing to the Mormon concept of divine revelation where *The Book of Mormon* is concerned, is found in 3d Nephi, chapter 11, verses 27 and 36. These two verses are a

---

[1] Because of this teaching the Mormon church discriminates against Negroes and refuses to ordain any of them to either of the priesthoods.

[2] *The Book of Abraham* has now been branded "an insult to the intelligence of the scientific community" by top Mormon Egyptologist Dee Jay Nelson, designated by the Church to translate the papyri found in 1966 and authenticated by the Church from its own copy which had been supressed for approximately 130 years.

direct paraphrase of I John 5:7 and its context, coupled with statements made by Jesus Christ and John the Baptist (*in perfect King James English*, and in the order placed by the King James translators), and this supposedly 1,200 years before there was such a translation! The writer of *The Book of Mormon* really outdid himself there, especially since almost all Greek scholars are agreed that I John 5:7 is an *interpolation* relative to the doctrine of the Trinity and is not found in any of the early Greek manuscripts, a fact which in no way deterred the writer of *The Book of Mormon* from including it for nothing else but for its surprise effect! [3]

The reader is urged, if still unconvinced that *The Book of Mormon* is a scholastic fraud, to compare I Corinthians 12:1-11 with Moroni, chapter 10, Isaiah 4 with II Nephi 14, and Isaiah 2 with II Nephi 12, where it is easily discernible that the writer of *The Book of Mormon* has plagiarized word for word from the King James Bible, and as previously noted in perfect Elizabethan English! Add to this the fact that there is no such language as "Reformed Egyptian Hieroglyphics," the language Smith claimed was engraved upon the golden plates, and the further fact that the original *Book of Mormon* is considerably different in places from today's version, indicating the need for a revision of the "Divine" revelation. This makes the whole matter rather clear if one values objective evidence and historical facts. There are also more than 3,900 changes in *The Book of Mormon* between the 1830 edition and the latest copies."

We may safely say then that one should place his faith in the verifiable truths of Scripture and leave forever to itself the pseudo-revelation that is the *Book of Mormon*.

THE ATONEMENT

The Mormon doctrine of the Atonement of Christ is vastly different than that which is clearly stated within the pages of Scripture.

---

[3] Another example of this type of error is 3rd Nephi 11:33, 34, which is almost a direct quote from Mark 16:16, a passage now known to be spurious (see RSV).

In Volume 3 of his *Journal of Discourses,* page 247, Brigham Young stated, "There is not a man or woman who violates covenants made with their God that will not be required to pay the debt. *The blood of Christ will never wipe that out. Your own blood must atone for it,* the judgments of the Almighty will come sooner or later, and every man and woman will have to atone for breaking covenants."

Enlarging upon this statement further in Volume 4, pp. 219-20, Young wrote, "All mankind love themselves: and let these principles be known by an individual, and he would be glad to have his blood shed . . . I could refer you to plenty of instances where men have been righteously slain, in order to atone for their sins. . . . This is loving our neighbor as ourselves; if he needs help, help him; and if he wants salvation and it is necessary to spill his blood on the earth in order that he may be saved, spill it."

Since Brigham Young was the successor to Joseph Smith, and his revelations and teachings are considered by Mormons today to be as binding as those of Smith, there is little doubt what the Mormon position is regarding redemption through the blood of Christ. According to Mormonism there are sins that the blood of Jesus Christ cannot atone for. The Scriptures clearly state, however, that "If we confess our sins, he is faithful and just to forgive us our sins and to cleanse us from *all* unrighteousness" (I John 1:9), and further: "If we walk in the light as he is in the light, we have fellowship one with the other and the blood of Jesus Christ God's Son cleanseth us from *all* sin" (I John 1:7).

Let us take heed, then, when Mormons speak of the doctrine of the Atonement which is a finite one made by a Jesus who can remove only *some* sins but not *all* sins, and is in reality "another Jesus" (II Cor. 11:4). We ought always to beware, then, of such perversions of the true Gospel of Christ though they be couched in similar terminology.

---

4 Italics ours.

ETERNAL SALVATION

We close our comments on this area of Mormon theology with the Mormon position on salvation. The Bible teaches that spiritual salvation is wholly by grace through faith independent of the deeds of the law (Eph. 2:8-11), and further that we are justified before God by faith, apart from works so that it is grace that saves through faith, which in turn produces works that bear witness to the efficacy of the saving faith (James 2).

Contrasted with this position Brigham Young in *Discourses of Brigham Young*, p. 157, stated: "Some of our old traditions teach us that a man guilty of atrocious and murderous acts may savingly repent when on the scaffold and upon his execution will hear the expression: 'Bless God, he has gone to heaven to be crowned in glory through the all redeeming merits of Christ the Lord!' This is all nonsense. Such a character will never see heaven."

To sum up the problem, briefly, salvation to Mormons is not a free gift from God, the result of grace wholly separate from works. It is something to be earned, for as Brigham Young put it, "Will the water [of Baptism] [5] of itself wash them [sins] away? No; but keeping the commandments of God will cleanse away the stain of sin" (*Discourses of Brigham Young,* p. 159).

The Mormon concept of salvation is *faith* plus *baptism* plus *works*.* The Scriptures teach that works are the natural outgrowth of regeneration and justify us before the world (James 2:21, 24), but they in no way merit or add to the efficacy of saving grace (Rom. 4:4, 5 and Eph. 2:8, 9).

Rejecting as it does the infinite atonement of the Lord Jesus Christ and holding the unbiblical doctrine of blood atonement Mormonism has repudiated all right to be called Christian, for if there is one thing the New Testament clearly teaches it is the fact that Christ's blood

---

[5] Brackets ours.

* *Mormon Doctrine,* Bruce R. McConkie, pp. 669-70.

cleanses from *all* sin, [6] and "neither is there salvation in any other, for there is none other name under heaven given among men, whereby we must be saved" (Acts 4:12).

In the twenty-third chapter of Luke, the Lord Jesus Christ promised the repentant thief, "Today shalt thou be with me in paradise" (vv. 39-43). One need only compare this with the previously quoted statement of Brigham Young in *Discourses of Brigham Young* to realize that Brigham Young taught to the contrary. The Bible teaches that there is salvation through repentance even when all hope appears to be lost. The ears of the Lord are ever open to the cries of the penitent, and "whosoever shall call upon the name of the Lord shall be saved" (Rom. 10:13).

Examination of the Mormon gospel has shown us that it is indeed "another gospel," and not the true, rejecting as it does the great biblical doctrines of the atonement of Christ and salvation by grace apart from the deeds of the law. Mormonism further rejects the doctrine of justification by faith, or as apostle James Talmage has put it, "The sectarian dogma of justification by faith *alone* has exercised an influence for *evil* since the early days of Christianity" (p. 120, *The Articles of Faith*, 1909).[7]

Apostle Talmage further wrote: "The written works adopted by the vote of the church as authoritative guide to faith and doctrine are . . . The Bible, The Book of Mormon, The Doctrine and Covenants, and The Pearl of Great Price" (*The Articles of Faith*, p. 5). So not only do Mormons reject the previously listed doctrines of Scripture but they supplement the authority of Scripture itself by adding to the Word of God new "revelations" from the

---

[6] Some Mormon missionaries will vigorously deny the Utah church's usage and homage to the "Inspired Version" as Smith's translation is known. The fact is, however, that well-informed Mormons always use it despite the fact that the Reorganized Church (their historic rivals) print it and it can be purchased in Salt Lake City.

[7] Emphasis ours.

pen of "Prophet" Smith, whose prophetic mantle today rests on the shoulders of President Kimball, present leader of the Mormon Church and the successor of Joseph Smith—both adversaries of historic Christianity.

Contemporary Mormonism in its doctrinal structure therefore presents an ever-multiplying challenge to the true Church of Jesus Christ. May we arise to face it and not only preach His Word with power but defend with equal vigor the truths of that Word against the inroads of Mormon theology.

CHAPTER THREE

The Mormon Masquerade

One of the basic premises of the Mormon doctrinal system is the contention of Joseph Smith that all religions except his are "wrong" and an "abomination" in God's sight. To dismiss doubt on this point, we refer the reader to the words of Joseph Smith himself whom all Mormons are bound to recognize as a prophet of God equal if not superior to any of the Old Testament prophets. Wrote "Prophet" Smith, recounting his alleged conversation with the Almighty at the age of 15, in the year 1820:

> My object in going to inquire of the Lord was to know which of all the sects was right, that I might know which to join. No sooner, therefore, did I get possession of myself, so as to be able to speak, than I asked the Personages who stood above me in the light, which of all the sects was right—and which I should join.
>
> I was answered that *I must join none of them, for they were all wrong*; and the Personage who addressed me said that *all their creeds were an abomination in his sight;* that *those professors were all corrupt;* that: "they draw near to me with their lips, but their hearts are far from me; they teach for doctrines the commandments of men, having

a form of godliness, but they deny the power thereof."

He again forbade me to join with any of them;[1] and many other things did he say unto me, which I cannot write at this time (*Pearl of Great Price*, J. S. 2:18-20).

In addition to this statement, Samuel W. Taylor, noted Mormon author, wrote in *The American Weekly* (April 3, 1955) in answer to the question, "Are Mormons Christians?" the following reply:

Yes, indeed—but neither Protestant nor Catholic. Mormons believe that there was a breaking away of the other churches from true Christianity and that their religion is the *restored* gospel.

From these facts, it is evident for all intelligent persons to see that Mormonism claims to be *the* true Christian religion complete with an exclusive message, infallible prophets and higher revelations for a new dispensation which the Mormons would have us believe began with Joseph Smith, Jr.

The Mormon masquerade has in recent years been most successful. Even the life of Brigham Young (historically a scoundrel of immense proportions) has been dramatized by Hollywood into a stirring syrupy motion picture of the same name glorifying Smith's immoral successor and carefully omitting his unsavory past (released under the title, "Brigham Young" in 1940, starring Dean Jagger, noted American actor). The Mormons however have been greatly aided in their propaganda efforts by two seldom considered factors: (1) The concept that people who "live good lives" and establish a religion that "lasts" must be "Christian people," and (2) the pitiful lethargy of the Christian Church in recognizing the great dangers of Mormonism and its failure to take steps to unmask, evangelize and combat it.

A very clear-cut example of point number one is found in Taylor's article in *The American Weekly* previously referred to. In answer to the question, "Was Joseph Smith a fraud?" Mr. Taylor answered: "Mormons answer this

---

[1] Italics ours.

by pointing to the fruits of Mormonism. Could a fraud, they ask, have established a church that would thrive under almost a century of unrelenting attack?"

The answer to Mr. Taylor's question is, of course, a most emphatic "yes"! And to prove the point one need only turn to the history of other religious charlatans among whom are Mary Baker Eddy (Christian Science), Charles and Myrtle Fillmore (Unity), Madam Blavatsky (Theosophy), and Charles Taze Russell (Jehovah's Witnesses), to mention just a few. The religions founded by these persons have also endured "great" persecutions, are apparently thriving, and are avowed enemies of historic Christianity. These religions incidentally are condemned as non-Christian by the Latter Day Saints themselves, so it is evident that if the Mormons regard persecution and endurance as a test of spiritual validity or reliability where religion is concerned, they must at length recognize the claims of their fellow cultists, and this they are most unwilling to do!

The New Testament painstakingly warns Christians not to be deceived by so-called "good lives" or "a form of godliness" (II Tim. 3:5) where people in general are concerned, but to "test the spirits" (I John 4:1) to see if they conform to sound doctrine which Mormonism, as has been shown, does not! We learn from Scripture that false prophets often duplicate through Satan the miracles of God (see Ex. 7:11, 22), and live exemplary lives that appear "good" but which in reality are devoid of the faith that saves (Eph. 2:8-11). The Lord Jesus Christ, it will be remembered, unmistakably taught that "*the* work of God" is "*to believe* on him whom God hath sent" (John 6:29), and this He said in direct answer to those who wanted to know how to do the "good" works of His Father. The Mormons then may appear Christian by human standards of judgment and their religion apparently productive of "good works" but underneath the veneer of professed Christianity lies the denial of "the only Lord God and our Lord, Jesus Christ" and the subtle substitution of "another gospel" (Jude 4, II Cor. 11:4).

THREE FUNDAMENTALS OF
HISTORIC MORMON THEOLOGY

In keeping with this aforementioned masquerade, the Mormons are not above resorting to blatant misrepresentation, a superb example of which is found in their guarded answers to a set of questions that *Look* magazine asked, the results of which were published in its famous series of articles on various religions. This concrete example of Mormon semantics is found in the October 5, 1954, edition of *Look* and has been reproduced in Leo Rosten's book, *A Guide to the Religions of America* (Simon & Schuster, New York, 1955, pp. 91-100), from which we have quoted the following material used. To simplify the reader's task of following the Mormons through the labyrinth of shifty language, which makes up their replies, we have chosen to state certain of the questions as they appeared in *Look* and give the Mormon answer followed by a brief documented statement entitled, "The Truth," portraying the real Mormon position according to their own literature and historical sources, etc. ·

I. The Doctrine of the Trinity

Question: Do Mormons believe in the Holy Trinity? (p. 93).

Answer: Yes. The Latter Day Saint accepts the Godhead as three literal, distinct personalities: God the Father; His Son, Jesus the Christ (who is one with the Father in purpose, and in thought, but separate from Him in physical fact); and the Holy Ghost, a Personage of spirit (Acts 7:55, etc.).

The Truth: Mormons have never historically and do not now accept the Christian doctrine of the Holy Trinity and Mr. Evans who answered *Look's* question knows it!* The question as it was asked to many spokesmen for the various religions (there were eighteen in all) referred directly to the historic orthodox Christian doctrine of the

---

*Holy Trinity—"Within the Nature of the one eternal God there are three Persons, the Father, the Son and the Holy Spirit."

Trinity as defined at Nicaea in 325 A.D., and as held by the Roman Catholic, Greek Orthodox, and other historically orthodox bodies. Mr. Evans also knew this if from nothing else other than the answers given by those whose articles preceded his own. In this relation, it is interesting to observe that M. G. Henschel (see p. 59 of Rosten) who wrote on the views of Jehovah's Witnesses (rabid anti-Trinitarians) knew exactly what *Look* meant when it spoke of the "Holy Trinity" and so did every other writer in the series who was queried. So we cannot accept the possibility that Mr. Evans misunderstood the question, seeing that he occupies such a responsible position in his own church.

This one alternative having been removed, it is increasingly apparent that Mr. Evans deliberately avoided giving his church's true position on the Trinity because he knows it is not accepted by any Christian denomination or church in the world, and is one of the major reasons why the Mormon Church has never been invited to join the National Council or World Council of Christian Churches or any orthodox church fellowships in Christendom.

The key to the Mormon doctrine of the Trinity is found in the words "but separate from Him in physical fact" as previously quoted from Mr. Evans' answer.

Joseph Smith, the Mormon prophet whose words all loyal Mormons are ruled by, once described the Trinity in the following terms:

> The Father has a body of flesh and bones as tangible as man's; the Son also; but the Holy Ghost has not a body of flesh and bones but is a personage of spirit . . . (*Doctrine and Covenants*, 130:22).

Corroborating Smith's unbiblical and unchristian concept of God, Brigham Young, the prophet's successor, wrote in his *Journal of Discourses* 1:50, the following elaboration on Smith's "revelation":

> When our father Adam came into the garden of Eden, he came into it with *a celestial body* and brought Eve, *one of his wives*, with him. . . . He *is our* Father *and our* God *and the only God with whom we have to do.**

---

*Italics theirs.

To dismiss any further doubt that the Mormons deliberately misrepresent their view of the Trinity so as to appear Christian, we cite Parley Pratt, noted Mormon theologian and contemporary of Smith and Young who wrote in his book, *Key to the Science of Theology* (p. 44, 1973 ed.), another refutation of the current Mormon masquerade. Wrote Mr. Pratt:

> Each of these Gods, including Jesus Christ and His Father, being in possession of not merely an organized spirit, but a glorious body of flesh and bones . . .

With the facts out in the open, it is evident for all to see that the Mormons are polytheists and anti-Trinitarians masquerading under Christian terminology in a clever attempt to appear as "angels of light" when in reality they are, as Paul describes them, "ministers of Satan" (II Cor. 11:14, 15). Mr. Evans' answer to *Look's* question on the Trinity then is strong evidence that scholastic dishonesty and semantic trickery are apparently standard Mormon practices in their ever expanding attempt to appear as Christians, which they are *not*! For the Christian then, "God is Spirit" (John 4:24) and Jesus Christ is His manifestation in flesh, truly "the image of the invisible God" (Col. 1:15), not one of a pantheon of polygamous gods as Mormon theology interprets Him.

II. The Virgin Birth of Christ

Question: Do Mormons believe in the Virgin Birth? (p. 94).

Answer: Yes. The Latter Day Saint accepts the miraculous conception of Jesus, the Christ.

The Truth: This second example of Mormon misrepresentation is just one more testimony to the fact that the Mormons dare not come out openly before the public at large and reveal their weird system of theology with its pseudo-similarity to the Christian Gospel. This they will not do because no informed person, even those with nominal Christian upbringing, could fail to grasp the significance of their theological term switching. Knowing this fact, the Mormons, as Mr. Evans has so capably demonstrated, give verbal assent to recognized Christian doctrines and prefer to first "sell" Mormonism as a religion by their apparent adherence to, and practice of, Christian principles before indoctrinating the unsuspecting convert into the labyrinth of antichristian dogmas which constitute Mormon theology.

That the Mormons deny the biblical account of the Virgin Birth of our Lord as recorded in Luke 1:26-35, no thorough student of the movement has ever denied, for in the words of Prophet Brigham Young:

> When the Virgin Mary conceived the child Jesus, the Father had begotten him in his own likeness. He was *not* begotten by the Holy Ghost. And who was the Father? He was the first of the human family (Adam); [2] ... Jesus, our elder brother, was begotten in the flesh by the same character that was in the garden of Eden, and who is our Father in Heaven" (*Journal of Discourses,* Vol. I, pp. 50, 51).

Mr. Evans in his "answer" to the question in *Look* should have stated the true position of his church, but knowing that Christians everywhere, not to mention the major denominations and the Roman Catholic Church as a body, would openly attack such a perverted and unscriptural view projected under the guise of Christianity by those who claim they are Christians,[3] the Mormon spokesman verbally assented to what he knew was *not,* and never has been, the position of his church. The only "miraculous conception" that historic Mormon theology reflects and genuine Mormons (those who obey Brigham Young's revelations) agree to is that Adam-god had sexual intercourse with the Virgin Mary, and that the result of this union produced Jesus Christ! [4] They do not,

---

[2] Parentheses are ours and are based upon Young's own statement " ... Adam is our Father and our God and the only God with whom we have to do."

[3] Though many debates have raged over the nature of the Virgin Birth of Christ, the orthodox position has always been based upon literal acceptance of Luke 1, etc., and even the dissenters repudiate in toto the Mormon concept.

[4] Talmadge's *Articles of Faith* (ed. 1924, pp. 472-473) inadvertently reveals this doctrine in the phrase which declares that Christ

as has been shown, and as the Bible teaches, believe that Christ was conceived by the Holy Spirit through a direct act of God independent of any sexual relationship; therefore, and as a result, their whole concept is shown to be a blasphemous derivation from the mythology of Greece coupled with unmistakable signs of pagan sexual perversions (i.e., the gods having intercourse with the daughters of men and begetting children, etc.), concepts that are totally foreign to the Bible they profess to believe in.

We leave to the judgment of the reader this further evidence of Mormon ethics, a deception that began with Joseph Smith and which today boldly masquerades itself as a Christian sect. The Mormons have also succeeded in deceiving *Life* magazine into believing that they are Christians (see *Life,* December, 1955), and thus classifying them with other Protestant denominations, all of whom consider the Mormons a non-Christian cult!

III. The Authority of the Bible

Question: What do Mormons believe about the Bible?

Answer: The Bible is basic to Mormon belief. The King James Version is officially used, and is believed to be "the Word of God" as far as it is translated correctly.

The Truth: The Mormon Church does *not* accept the Bible as "*the* Word of God" as Mr. Evans so casually states it, but adds to the Scriptures other "books": (1) The Book of Mormon, (2) Doctrine and Covenants, (3) The Pearl of Great Price. These "inspired writings" are declared to be of *equal* authority with the Bible, despite the fact that they not only contradict Scripture in numerous places but *each other* as well! (Compare *Doctrine and Covenants,* sec. 132, vs. 1, with *The Book of Mormon,* Jacob 2:23, 24).

---

was unique, "offspring of a mortal mother and of an immortal, or resurrected, and glorified, Father." In the original 1899 edition of Talmadge the quote did not appear. It was added later and then moved to the rear of the text.

The old Mormon dodge regarding "correct" translation of the Scriptures is also utilized by the disciples of Prophet Smith, who use it as their "loophole" of escape whenever the Scriptures puncture one of their pet teachings, as is so often the case. When a nasty situation of that type arises, however, the Mormons are usually quite equal to it and will claim the offending Scripture "incorrectly translated" despite the fact that scarce indeed is the Mormon or missionary in 25,000 who could exegete or translate the Old or New Testaments using the original languages were his very soul to depend upon it, and they know it!

So whenever the "correctly translated" phrase is utilized in Mormon literature or in conversation with Mormons, Christians should recognize it for what it is, a clever denial of the sole authority of Scripture and a recognition of other extra-biblical authorities, namely, the writings of Joseph Smith, Brigham Young and the succeeding line of Mormon "prophets."

ADDING TO THE WORD OF GOD

On the subject of authority it should also be noted that Joseph Smith allegedly began a revision of the Bible under "Divine Inspiration" but his sudden death left the work incomplete. A sample of how "prophet" Smith went about "revising" God's Word is found in Smith's translations of John 1:18 and I John 4:12.

In his vain attempt to improve upon the inspiration of the Holy Spirit Smith wrote:

> And no man hath seen God at any time, *except he hath borne record of the Son,* for except it is through him no man can be saved (John 1:18).

> No man has seen God at any time, *except them who believe.* If we love one another, God dwells in us, and His love is perfected in us" (I John 4:12). [5]

Any cursory comparison of the New Testament Greek

---

[5] Recorded in: Le Grand Richard's *A Marvelous Work and a Wonder* (Salt Lake City: The Deseret Book Co., 1950), pp. 18, 19.

at these verses, or for that matter, any sound English translation quickly reveals that Smith inserted the two above italicized phrases in a bungling attempt to back up his manufactured revelation of God as a physical being not a Spirit as the Bible teaches (John 4:24). Apostle Le Grand Richards, of the Mormon Church attempts to prove that very thing in his book, *A Marvelous Work and a Wonder* (p. 19), showing that for Mormons, the Bible *alone* is *not* the Word of God. In fact, careful study will reveal that it cannot logically be God's Word at all where the Mormons are concerned, for they very often contradict it and openly supplement it at will with their three previously mentioned pseudo-revelations, and wherever it suits them, ignore Scripture as "incorrectly translated." Smith apparently was either oblivious to the expressed warning against adding *to* or subtracting *from* the Word of God, or willfully disobedient to it (see Rev. 22:18, 19). At any rate he clearly transgressed God's revealed will and all loyal Mormons who follow his example continue in his transgression. [6]

Considering these facts, then, it is clear that once more Mr. Evans has neglected to tell the whole story for the obvious reason that a half-truth is safer than a complete falsehood, and the Mormons have historically clung to half-truths from Smith and Young to Evans and Kimball, their now presiding president.

We should view with suspicion, then, any published statements from Mormon sources where the foundational doctrines of the Gospel are concerned; since, as has been shown, they have not in the past hesitated to employ deception in their effort to mimic orthodox Christianity (which orthodoxy they have been and are today in diametric opposition to). Therefore let us not be deceived. Rather let us recognize their errors, pray for their re-

---

[6] Many Mormons attempt to escape the clear implication of Young's statement limiting the power of Christ's blood by pointing out that a criminal is executed to "atone" for his crimes and this is all Brigham Young meant. But Young's statement declares that what Christ's blood could *not* cleanse a man's own blood atonement *could* so the whole subterfuge fails completely.

demption, and overcome their false teachings in the power and through the Gospel of Jesus Christ.

Conclusion

In the final analysis we ought to recognize Mormonism for what it is, a cleverly designed counterfeit of the Christian religion, and we ought never to forget that Mormonism always puts its best foot forward. The fact was clearly demonstrated when the then Secretary of Agriculture, Ezra Taft Benson, a high Mormon leader and one of the vaunted 12 Apostles, appeared with his family on a national television program. Throughout the whole broadcast Secretary Benson exemplified the "down to earth" religious family man typical of the so-called "Mormon heritage," and was a sparkling advertisement for the Mormon faith.

But underneath the filmy coat of pseudo-Christian testimony Benson and all Mormons adhere tenaciously to the anti-Christian dogmas of Joseph Smith and Brigham Young. It is to the distinct advantage, then, of all sincere students that they examine carefully the unvarnished doctrines of the Mormon cult that they be not deceived by mere "appearances" and "forms of godliness."

Paul the Apostle warns us that Satan sometimes disguises himself as "an angel of light" and his servants or emissaries do likewise (II Cor. 11:13-15). Let us remember these things well in this age of ever-deepening doctrinal apostasy, that we be not deterred in either our profession or defense of the faith that saves (Eph. 2:8-11).

CHRISTIAN RESEARCH INSTITUTE

Through the publication of tracts and pamphlets, all interested Christian pastors, teachers, and workers will receive reliable, documented information on the major cults, a pioneer missionary research effort never before attempted on an international, interdenominational basis.

For the first time in the history of Christian missions, it will be possible to keep a running commentary on the activities of all major sects, American and foreign. Missionaries will be apprised of the methods of cult infiltration and provided with answers to oppose this growing problem.

The opportunity to constructively meet this challenge now stands available to the Christian Church through the facilities of CRI. For the first time, there is a chance to effectively answer the cults and present them with the Gospel in a context of enlightened and equipped Christian workers "speaking the truth in love."

Further information about CRI and its many services may be obtained by writing to its headquarters at P.O. Box 500, San Juan Capistrano, California 92675.

BIBLIOGRAPHY

Arbaugh, H. B., *Revelations in Mormonism* (Chicago: University of Chicago Press, 1932).

Boyd, Robert F., *Mormonism*.

Brodie, Fawn M., *No Man Knows My History* (Alfred A. Knopf, 1946).

Brooks, Juanita, *The Mountain Meadows Massacre* (Stanford: Stanford University Press, 1943).

Clark, Elmer T., *The Small Sects in America* (New York: Abingdon-Cokesbury, 1949).

Clark, J. A., *Gleanings By the Way* (1842).

Evans, J. H. *One Hundred Years of Mormonism* (Salt Lake City: Deseret News, 1905).

Evans, R. C., *Forty Years in the Mormon Church, Why I Left* (1920).

Ferguson, Charles W., *New Books of Revelation* (New York: Doubleday-Doran Co., Inc., 1929), chapter on Mormonism.

Gerstner, John, *The Theology of the Major Sects* (Grand Rapids: Baker Book House, 1960).

Interpretation Magazine, article, "Bible and Modern Religions," Vol. 10, No. 4 (1956), pp. 440-446.

Linn, William Alexander, *The Story of the Mormons* (New York: Macmillan Co., 1902).

Martin, Walter R., *The Rise of the Cults* (Grand Rapids: Zondervan, 1955).

———, *The Christian and the Cults* (Grand Rapids: Zondervan, 1956).

Mead, Frank S., *Handbook of Denominations* (New York: Abingdon-Cokesbury, 1955).

Richards, Le Grand, *A Marvelous Work and a Wonder* (Salt Lake City: Deseret Book Co., 1950).

Schaff-Herzog *Encyclopedia of Religious Knowledge*, Vol. 8 (Grand Rapids: Baker Book House, 1953).

Smith, Joseph, Jr., *The Book of Mormon* (Salt Lake City: The Church of Jesus Christ of Latter Day Saints, 1952).

———, *Doctrine and Covenants* (Salt Lake City: The Church of Jesus Christ of Latter Day Saints).

———, *The Pearl of Great Price* (Salt Lake City: The Church of Jesus Christ of Latter Day Saints, 1953).

Snowden, James H., *The Truth About Mormonism* (New York: George H. Durant Co., 1926).

Stenhouse, T. B., *The Rocky Mountain Saints* (New York: B. Appleton Co., 1873).

Tucker, Pomeroy, *Origin, Rise and Progress of Mormonism* (1867).

Talmage, James E., *The Articles of Faith* (Salt Lake City: The Church of Jesus Christ of Latter Day Saints, 1952).

Taylor, John, *The Mediation and Atonement* (The Church of Jesus Christ of Latter Day Saints).

VanBaalen, J. K., *The Chaos of Cults* (Grand Rapids: Eerdmans, 1956), revised edition.

Widtsoe, John A., *Discourses of Brigham Young* (1973).

Young, Ann Eliza, *Wife No. 19, A Life in Bondage* (1876).

Young, Brigham, *Journal of Discourses*, Vol. 1 (1854).